Your Expensive Mortgage: How The HAMP Plan and Other Options Can Help You!

John H. Bauer
Attorney at Law

"Your Expensive Mortgage: How the HAMP Plan and Other Options Can Help You!"

This book is intended for instructional purposes only and is intended to provide accurate and authoritative information with regard to the subject matter covered. Please note, however, that foreclosure and eviction laws differ from state to state. As a result, it is not possible to cite each and every law and how it may apply to your own individual situation in your own state where you reside. Your individual situation is unique. We have attempted to provide you with general principles which you should consider when making a decision regarding keeping or giving up your home. Where specific legal, tax, or other expert assistance is required, the services of a competent professional in your own state should be sought.

Please note that the HAMP loan modification plan is a federal program. It's requirements have been established by the federal government and therefore should apply equally and properly to citizens of each and every state within the U.S.A. Other loan modification programs may differ from state to state depending upon the identity of the loan servicer, the loan servicer's investor, or the purchaser of the mortgage note from the lender.

The author, printers, licensees, and distributors make no warranties, express or implied, about the merchantability or fitness for any particular use of this product.

You can also visit our website: www.gr8tsupport.com; or call us directly at (714) 319-3446.

Your Expensive Mortgage: How the HAMP Plan and Other Options can Help You!

TABLE OF CONTENTS:

LIST OF EXHIBITS (5):

Exhibit "A": HAMP Loan Modification Application from a Major National Lender.

Exhibit "B": Sample Budget Worksheet to be included in Loan Mod Application.

Exhibit "C": Sample "Hardship Letter" to be included in Loan Mod Application in order to seek a Loan Modification.

Exhibit "D": Sample "Hardship Letter" to be included in Loan Mod Application in order to seek a Short Sale.

Exhibit "E": Sample "Hardship Letter" to be included in Loan Mod Application in order to seek a "Deed in Lieu of Foreclosure."

FOREWARD

I am writing this book in the midst of one of the most serious financial crises in the history of our nation. I see this everyday in the midst of my legal practice in California. I am a licensed attorney in the state of California and maintain a Chapter 11 bankruptcy practice. I have to deal with mortgage lenders every and every day, both on a pre and post bankruptcy basis.

I'm telling you right here and now: you can do a lot of good work with your lender, keep your home, and never have to go to court or consider filing bankruptcy. That's the purpose of this book—help you handle your "expensive" mortgage and never go to court, get dragged into court, or have to file bankruptcy because of that mortgage.

Although this is not a book about bankruptcy, you may ask what is a "Chapter 11" bankruptcy? What does he do for a living? A Chapter 11 bankruptcy is a legal means to reorganize your personal and business debt with the goal being that you keep your properties and keep your business running as a going concern, rather than liquidating your business and going home. A Chapter 7 bankruptcy on the other hand is a "liquidation" bankruptcy. Although you may be able to keep certain property, you are pretty much throwing up your hands and saying: "I give up. I want to start over."

In my "reorganization" practice, the idea is to get an agreement and a viable Plan of reorganization. That's what this book is about: taking a look at your financial options with your mortgage and deciding which option is the best for you. These options include "reorganizing" your debt in the sense of making new agreements with your mortgage lender. Some options include "liquidating" your mortgage debt *without bankruptcy* because there isn't a realistic way for you continue to make the payments and keep the home. You do need to get out.

In my practice, I have obtained formal orders from the bankruptcy court that lenders must accept hundreds of thousands of dollars less for their mortgages than the original mortgage notes provide. In some cases, I have gotten the lenders to agree to take hundreds of thousands of dollars less because it makes economic sense for the lender to do so—rather than take a huge loss from the foreclosure sale—or get the deal crammed down their throats by the Court.

One of the methods of negotiating with these lenders is the loan modification. I have prepared loan modification applications for clients—without the filing of any accompanying bankruptcy—and have also sought modifications within the bankruptcy process. In either case, the loan modification is a "reorganization" effort on your part. If you can get your payments reduced, you can keep the property. If not, you may need to liquidate because your "overall picture" doesn't support the debt you have.

I also speak about your "liquidation" options for your mortgage in this book, options that you may have without the need to ever file any bankruptcy. That's the purpose of this book—tell you about some options you have without the need to ever file any bankruptcy!

If you have a challenge with your home or rental property mortgage, you're certainly not alone. Tough economic times, lower salaries, adjustable rate mortgages, and layoffs are all contributing to the need to take a careful look at your first, most important asset, your home with its' mortgage, and determining how you can make this part of your budget work for you…

That's all well and good to discuss the bad economy, but the critical question is how do I and all of us deal with this economy? The purpose of this book is to do just that! One of the biggest challenges underlying our economy is the housing sector and, more particularly, addressing your personal questions: What can I do with my house? What can I do with my expensive mortgage loan? What rationale can I use to make the best decisions for myself and my family? Should I take the emotional hit that a foreclosure will incur upon me and my family? Do I really need to take that kind of a hit? How do I minimize the potentially negative consequences of a mortgage that I can no longer afford to pay? What options do I have with my "bad" or "expensive" mortgage?

This is the simple fact: "winners" have options. The purpose of this book is to make you a true "winner" in the midst of this serious mortgage crisis. The purpose of this book is to explain to you your potential options. When you review your options, you have the information necessary to make the very best decision for <u>you</u>. This decision is different for everyone. So I'm going to talk about a lot of different options which include both keeping your home and strategically giving up your home so that you are in the best, strongest position to fight another day!

I will discuss some different clients and their cases with whom I have specifically worked in the past, what decisions we arrived at, how we executed our decisions to get the very best result, and what happened as a result.

I will also discuss a couple cases where the people went ahead and make "bad" decisions and what resulted. I provide you with "what could have been" scenarios if only the home owner had acted properly, prudently, and within the rules.

Once you understand the "rules" of the mortgage game, you can make the very best decision. Now, let's take a look at some real people and how the "rules" applied to them so you can see where you fit in!

Chapter 1: Saving Your Home! Your Loan Modification Option

I. A Story from the Darkside

I remember when I was sitting in my office one day and a lady called my wife and asked her if we could help her to try to save her home from foreclosure.

I thought to myself: "I'd really like to help her. I know she doesn't have any money. I'd feel real good about myself if I could help."

So, our friend came to the house where I had my office and laid down a lot of paperwork. She really didn't have the first idea of how to help herself. She didn't even have any paperwork from her bank, but she said she was in foreclosure and wanted to see if she could get a "loan modification."

I had helped a number of people with their loan mods and thought to myself: "Let's hope that her numbers work right for her." This home was her principal residence (where she lived) so I knew I might have a good shot since many banks are part of the national HAMP program to help homeowners with their mortgage payments. This is the program that was started by President Obama.

One of the reasons that this program works is that the banks and loan servicers are actually paid by the federal government for participating in the modification program and agreeing to loan modifications.

First, I asked her for her bank application for the mod. She promptly told me: "I don't have any application. I can never get through to the Bank. I keep talking to collectors over there that won't help me."

Does this sound familiar to you? It might if you have ever spent your time trying to talk to any one from a lender customer service department. In some instances, these people make a total shambles of the concept of "customer service". I don't know how many of these people get hired in the first place, but I'm sure that some of them are not paid well and not trained well—except to pump you for a lot of personal information…personal information that you were going to give them anyway if you could just get that darn loan mod application!!! In some instances, you might get a very helpful person to talk to.

Well, fortunately, she did know the name of the Bank. I looked up the website of the Bank and found a link to a complete loan modification application. Eureka! The keys to the kingdom were within my reach. I pulled the papers down and started to figure out how this lady's numbers could earn her a sparkling new lower and more affordable mortgage payment.

Remember, if you can't get an application because you—like many others—cannot have a meaningful conversation with one of those 1-800 lender geeks, just go to the lender website and pull down the application and start from there. It's better for your piece of mind if you do this anyway. If you have to talk to them, however, they generally belong to the "loss mitigation" department. Just file that for later and use it only if absolutely necessary.

Sometimes your lender will go ahead and send you an application and actually invite you to apply for a loan modification. This means that the lender already recognizes that you have a problem with your loan…you should definitely take them up on the invitation!

When I went through her paperwork, I calculated her actual "self employed" income (this is sometimes a trick if you are self-employed) and figured out reasonable expenses for each expense category in the Application.

See Exhibit A (in the back of this book) which is a complete HAMP loan modification application provided on the internet by a national lender. Pages 5 and 7 of that Application provide you the budget forms to list your monthly income and projected monthly expenses. Start reviewing this form. This will be an important form for you. Exhibit B is a sample, filled out budget form for your review.

When you're an employed person, you merely list your monthly gross income on the budget form and attach a copy of a couple of your most recent pay stubs to prove what you are saying in the Application.

When you're a "self employed" person, the bank will typically ask you to prepare a Quarterly Profit & Loss Statement" which involves calculating what you made over the last 3 months and deducting your business expenses from that amount to conclude with what amounts to your real "gross income." You then deduct your personal expenses from that income to determine how much you really have left over to pay a mortgage.

This is critical. You need to know this. When you prepare a budget for the lender (income and expenses), it must show a NEGATIVE NUMBER at the bottom when you put in your current mortgage payments.

Undeniable Truth No. 1

If you prepare one of these budgets for the bank and it shows a positive number with your existing mortgage, you're automatically not entitled to a loan modification because you *can pay* your existing mortgage.

_____

In my friends' case, her monthly mortgage was about $1250. per month. Yes, it was a small mortgage—but all of these same principles apply and I'll prove it when we speak about much larger home mortgages.

After discussing her expenses with her, we were able to get a slight positive budget IF her mortgage payment became $738. per month which is about 59% of her existing mortgage, using the 2% interest rate that the HAMP program uses to calculate affordable payments. Let me tell you—I was very happy. This was possible.

Next, we had to look at what percentage this mortgage payment of $738. was of her monthly gross income (before deducting taxes and expenses). One goal of the gov't program is to limit the monthly mortgage payment to about 31% of the borrower's monthly gross income. In this case, the new mortgage payment of $738. per month was about 31% of what she showed she was earning each month, about $2380. per month.

So, I liked this modification. I prepared the necessary accompanying "Hardship Letter" which I will explain later and gathered up the other paperwork the lender wanted and asked her to mail the materials directly to their desired address.

The "hardship letter" explains why things have gotten so tough for the borrower, why she can no longer pay the original mortgage that she started out with. This letter will explain loss of income, increased expenses, illness in family, adjustable rate mortgage which has unduly raised the payments, and just about anything else that could negatively impact that borrower's ability to consistently and timely pay the original mortgage. You'll see a copy of a form "hardship letter" to obtain a loan mod attached as Exhibit C to this book.

Well, about a month later (a month later! Quick response!), she calls us and joins us out at dinner and shows us the letter from her bank, Wells Fargo, approving her new loan modification at $738. per month for a 3 month trial period (will talk about this later). Now, her financial situation would be much improved and she could keep her nice 4 bedroom house and yard in a suburb of Phoenix, Arizona if she could properly follow through with the Bank.

Actually, she was approved for a 3 month trial modification. Under the HAMP plan, this is what typically happens. Before the lender will give you a permanent modification, it will give you a 3 month trial modification. *Theoretically*, if you make each of your 3 specified payments in a timely fashion (not even one day late!!), the lender should send you a permanent loan modification for roughly the same monthly payment.

I say *theoretically* because, frankly, some lenders are not offering the permanent modification even after the borrower properly follows through with the trial modification. You just can't predict what your particular lender will do with you so you timely send them the specified payments each month during the trial modification with the earnest expectation that the bank will offer you a permanent mod…and hope for the best.

The letter from the bank that my client received also said to submit some additional paperwork by the date of the first payment which was in about a month, along with the first payment for $738. Simple enough!

The next time I see her she says that she never sent in the materials to the bank and she'd lost her mod and didn't want to keep the house anyway.

I share this story with you because it definitely made an impression on me. I was very sad and couldn't imagine why someone wouldn't pay enough attention to submit the additional, necessary documents to their bank and try to keep their house.

Sometimes the reason people don't get their loan mods is because they don't "finish". They don't send the final documents requested by the bank back to the bank in order to continue with the process and get approved for a permanent modification.

Undeniable Truth No. 2

When you apply for one of these mods, you have to read what the lender tells you. If it says that it needs some additional materials, you send them. The fact is that you might have properly included them in your package the first time. The fact is, however, that these banks lose much of what you send them so send them again BECAUSE THE BANK SAYS SO!

Also, make your new payment when they tell you to do so! Don't ignore what the bank tells you. If you don't follow the bank's instructions to the letter, you may lose your mod and have to rent an apartment or live in someone's house as a renter. Bad result!

_____

This was a mod that went bad because the person didn't care enough to be careful for some strange reason. I'll never figure it out.

The fact is that these lenders typically have so much red tape and bureaucracy involved in granting these loan mods that you can virtually never change their minds about rescinding their denial decision because you screwed up!

Later, I got a call from her friend asking me to help her move out of her house which was being foreclosed and I told him: "No, I don't want to help her leave the home that I helped her save! There is no good reason that she's moving at all."

Later I heard that she had a downward change in circumstances and wasn't earning as much as she wrote in her loan modification application. So she let the house go because she couldn't pay the $738. per month. This is my reply to that: She had a 4 bedroom home. Why couldn't she rent one room in that house for just $300. or two rooms for $600. per month? If she had done that, she would have had either a $438. per month or $138. per month mortgage to pay! You can't get any kind of apartment (that you would want to live in) for less than those amounts.

A. Should You Give Up Your Home Because You're "Underwater" on Your Mortgage?

Another excuse I heard she made was that she was "underwater" on the house. The mortgage was higher than the property's value. Boy, I guess she thought that she was in a truly unique situation..hah!

This is my response to that: if you can get the bank to agree to a loan modification which is about the same or less than rent, you better take it. In this lady's case, she had a decent sized four bedroom house with a big eating area and kitchen and good sized back yard. She was going to pay $738. per month, less the amounts she received from anyone who rented any rooms there.

Her alternative was to rent an apartment. It couldn't be very big if she were to pay less than what she needed to pay to keep the house. She would have to go through the genuine inconvenience of moving her things and terrible despair in losing her home. She wouldn't own the property. She probably couldn't keep her dog. She couldn't fix the place up BECAUSE SHE DIDN'T OWN IT. Based upon these circumstances, how could renting be better than keeping and owning her own home? How was letting that house go back to the bank better than keeping that home and keeping her life together.

These factors don't even take into consideration that a person's self-esteem and self-worth must be hurt when he or she loses their home. There's no ifs or buts about that. With a hurt self-esteem, isn't it even more difficult to be happy in your life and move forward to be successful? It's going to take some time to feel better and it won't be immediate.

So, in conclusion, why take the big personal hit to your happiness by letting your home go back to the bank when you could keep yourself and your family in your home, even if you are "underwater" with the mortgage? The answer to me is obvious—you shouldn't take the hit.

Also, one final thing—have you ever thought how your credit will look after the foreclosure? Some apartments may not be willing to rent to you because you will have "bad credit". I can't sell this concept too highly because, frankly, I think the issue of personal credit is overrated in this depressive economy, but many apartments still use it so I thought I needed to mention it to you.

Also, just a note to inform you if you didn't know already—future banks will use your credit report and "fico score" as a means to *punish* you in the future because you couldn't or didn't follow their demands for payment.

Also, if you're in the process of foreclosure with a bank, don't let your expectations soar too high about buying a car either. When the auto dealer runs your credit and sees an open foreclosure, they will look at the listed mortgage and figure that into your expenses to see whether you qualify to make your car payment. They may determine that you don't qualify to buy the car, that you can't afford the car, because of that high mortgage payment—even though you're not making that payment. Thought you should know.

I want to finish this story by taking the facts from the unfortunate and ridiculous to the sublime...Our friend moved out of her house before the final foreclosure date. After the bank foreclosed on the home and sold the home to a third party at the foreclosure auction, she was heard to have said: "I'm so pleased. The home sold on the first day!"

Frankly, after hearing that story, I'm sorry that I ever helped her with any numbers at all or that I ever got a whiff of the loan application with the bank. This one was very hard for me to swallow.

B. One Way to Turn this Story Around (a bit)! How to Minimize Your loss If Your Loan Mod Doesn't Work Out

Since we're talking about a "darkside" story, I want to mention one way to turn this around a bit (as much as it can under the circumstances) to make this a "look at the brightside story!" I know you're probably saying that it is impossible to turn this story around; it's impossible to get anything positive out of this. I have to agree, but I need to add that there are a couple of things that she *could have done* which would have made her life much more pleasant and lucrative rather than just being happy the home sold in foreclosure "the first day".

These things include: (1) stay in the home as long as she possibly could legally and (2) when she got served with an eviction notice from the new buyer, to make an offer to the new owner that she would leave promptly and leave the home in nice, broom swept condition if she received some cash from the buyer. This is called "cash for keys". It is used often by tenants and owners when the properties have been foreclosed by lenders. The new owner can be the lender itself or the owner who bought the property at the lender's foreclosure auction. (3) Ask the new owner if he wanted her to stay there as his first renter with him.

If the new owner wanted her to move, how about asking for $2000. or $3000. to leave in a week or 10 days? There's certainly nothing wrong with that. Isn't that better for the new owner than taking the risk that the occupant is going to have to be evicted or that the occupant will file bankruptcy which could seriously delay the state eviction process or that the occupant will actively trash the place before moving?

DO NOT GET ME WRONG HERE. I would never advocate that any occupant of any premises ever damage the premises that they don't own anymore. In fact, such an action of "malfeasance" may be deemed a crime in many if not all jurisdictions and is certainly a basis for civil action probably everywhere. So, it's not smart, not proper, and not legal to deliberately harm or damage someone else's property.

You do need to consider this question, however, from the point of view of the new owner. How much is it worth to the new owner to have the security of getting his property back in fit condition? That's why it's good for an occupant who is soon to be a non-occupant to request some cash from the new owner and sign a written contract to the effect of moving, a time, condition of the property, and the amount of cash to be transferred from the owner to the soon to be non-occupant. This just makes good business sense.

In our case, our friend made a number of mistakes that could have made this a little better: she moved before the foreclosure. Why? Why? Why?

A basic fact is that some lenders file a notice of default on the home or even set a foreclosure sale date, but then don't follow through with the sale on the specific date. This may not happen often, depending upon where you live and the size of your loan, but, if it does happen—you moved while you still own the property. Now, you have to pay someone to stay somewhere while you could have stayed in your own home.

I knew someone who received a notice of default on their home in California. The home was part of a gated Home Owner Association. The foreclosure papers were posted all over the front gate leading into the complex. After that messy posting of papers, the bank did not actually schedule a foreclosure sale until about 1 year later!! During that time, the owner remained in the home, saved a lot of rent for himself, and actually even rented out some empty rooms to accumulate some more income…Great approach!

If the foreclosure sale is actually scheduled, the owner can call the trustee's tel. no. that he receives with the foreclosure notice and find out the sale date (and whether it changes), the minimum bid for the property, and, afterwards, *whether it really sold or whether the sale was put off.*

Please note also that you may be able to stop the foreclosure sale by applying for a loan modification—even though you come in late. I knew of another client who had a specific sale date set, faxed in a loan modification application to the lender, then called the trustee who was holding the sale to hear: "The sale has been postponed because the loan is being considered for a loan modification at this time."

*What this tells you is: don't give up! It's never too late to file a loan modification application with a bank and move towards keeping your home.

On the other hand, if the foreclosure sale has already occurred, you have some more time that you can stay in your home. In this case, she definitely should have waited until the lender or new buyer gave her <u>written notice to move</u>.

If the new buyer had served her with an eviction notice, that would have been a perfect time to speak to the owner and come to an agreement when she would be leaving. That would have been the perfect time to make an agreement of "cash for keys".

Also, in the case of a new private owner, that owner—if he's not planning to "flip" the property—might like the old owner to stay in the home as its first tenant with him. Wouldn't it be better to talk to the new owner about staying there? Isn't that better than being forced to move into some horrible apartment somewhere? Doesn't that help to minimize the shock of what just happened? All of these questions can be answered with a resounding "yes".

If the old owner can't stay, the new owner gets the property in decent, broom swept condition and the old owner gets some money to move forward with her life. Much more of a "win win" situation here, at least in the context of this type of event. Unfortunately, I didn't see any of that happen in this case.

C. Understand the HAMP Loan Modification Plan!

My CPA had me meet with one of his clients in his office to discuss the possibility of filing a bankruptcy. In looking through their finances, I asked them: "If you reduced your house payment in half from $4500. per month, would that make a huge difference in your finances? Do you think you could make it without filing bankruptcy? The wife and her husband told me a resounding "Yes". I told them that I would help them.

They told me that their home loan was with a major lender for $685,000. and that they had a second loan for $100,000. on the home. We agreed that we would start working together to prepare a loan modification application to their bank. I asked them to pull a loan modification application, as a start, out of the website for their lender.

Undeniable Truth No. 3:

Virtually every lender will have a loan mod application which you can pull right out of their website. Then you have all the documents you need to make your case to the lender to reduce your mortgage!

Well, I emailed her later to start our communication because she wouldn't respond to me. Later, she finally called me to tell me that she had "spoke with her lender and that she didn't qualify for the loan modification" and that "her loans were over $729,000" and so she didn't qualify for a modification and that "the lender told her to call HUD for help."

Frankly, there wasn't anything right about what she said. First, when she was referring to the amount of $729,000.—she was referring to the upper limit of a loan value for an Obama HAMP home loan modification. Actually, that limit is $729,750.

That's the official federal loan modification program which has actually been helping a lot of people to reduce their mortgage payments. The requirements in short are as follows:

(1) Owner Occupied Home
(2) Loan is $729,750 or less.
(3) Owner has a hardship—good reason he or she can't pay the regular mortgage.
(4) Loan is a Fannie Mae or Freddie Mac loan.

It's easy to understand no. 1 through no. 3 above. No. 4 may be a bit more difficult. The easiest way to see whether this is true is just call the lender you're paying and ask them whether they would do a HAMP loan for your house…if they say "yes", the loan is a Fannie Mae or Freddie Mac loan and you don't have to worry about the terminology.

If you qualify for one of these, you may get an interest rate reduction down to 2% fixed for 5 years. Also, the bank may reduce your payment to as low as 31% of your Gross Income—your income before you deduct income taxes.

Each lender that participates in this program can use its' own percentage of your gross income, but typically it runs about 31 to 34%.

Here's an incredible feature of this loan modification. If your current loan balance is too high for you to support at just 31% of your gross income, the lender may still schedule this payment for you which will then pay *only part of the loan*. The rest of the loan will be put aside for lack of a better term ("deferred") for you to pay off later.

Here's how this works: if your loan is $700,000. (under the HAMP maximum of $729,750.), but 31% of your gross income, using a 2% interest rate, would not pay that loan, the bank will look for the amount of loan that the 31% would pay at an interest rate of 2%.

For example, if it determined that the 31% pays a loan of $500,000. only, it could approve your modification—you would be paying off the loan of $500,000. and the bank would merely defer the remaining $200,000. You wouldn't be making a monthly payment on that remaining amount! I love the flexibility of this program—when it works.

In one specific case where the total loan amount was $494,000., the bank—using this program—divided the loan into two components: (1) the amount of $323,000., at 2% interest that was being paid on each month and (2) the amount of $171,000. that was being deferred.

This is the exact language of the modified note: "$171,000. of the new principal balance shall be deferred (the Deferred Principal Balance) and I will *not pay interest or make monthly payments on this amount.*"

"The new Principal Balance less the Deferred Principal Balance shall be referred to as the "Interest Bearing Principal Balance" and this amount is $323,000. Interest at the rate of 2% will begin to accrue on the Interest Bearing Principal Balance on 8/1/2010."

Thusly, even if your income has been reduced due to this real estate depression, I would strongly recommend that you seek one of these modifications for your principal home. You might be surprised at how good a deal you can get! And keep your home!!

So, you can see, my client above didn't understand how good this modification could be and she was finding all kinds or reasons not to act because she didn't have her facts straight!! DON'T STOP YOURSELF!! GET YOUR FACTS STRAIGHT AND MOVE FORWARD TO SAVE YOUR HOME!!

When you seek to modify your first loan, don't total all the loans you have to see if you qualify. Just look at your first loan—her first loan was $685,000. So, atleast from a loan balance standpoint, she still qualified for the modification.

BUT she went ahead and added the balance from

the second loan to make it $785,000. so she didn't qualify!! Mistake. That lender she spoke with really mixed her up. The only loan balance she had to be concerned about was the balance of the first loan.

Remember when I spoke previously about the lender "customer service" (sometimes "customer dis-service") department. This was a prime example of just that kind of disservice to a customer who was trying to save her home.

Next, she said she went over her numbers *on the phone* with the bank. I asked her in my email to her: "What numbers did you use? For what expenses?" She couldn't answer any of my questions.

Undeniable Truth No. 4:

Never go over your numbers with the lender live on the telephone unless you have <u>carefully</u> looked at the bank's budget form and filled in those numbers <u>in advance</u> so you feel sure and very comfortable with those numbers.

Also, if you actually "go over numbers on the telephone", make sure you know what those numbers actually were and for what category of expenses they applied. You need to have a clear record of what you discussed and the numbers you used.

———————————

Groceries: $450. per month

Cable: $110. per month

The problem with our client is that she didn't know what she said and she didn't know why she didn't qualify. There are better places for me to start as a professional. I don't like to start at a place like that.

If you have a first and second loan, the only balance that matters is the balance of your <u>first loan.</u> Don't add your first and second loan balance to determine whether you're under $729,750.!! She did that here.

In a later email to her, I also told her that, if she doesn't qualify for a HAMP modification, that she may still qualify to a conventional modification…so don't give up the ship. She may still get some lender help here.

I never heard from her again…

D. <u>Look at the HAMP in action!</u>

I have some clients who purchased the most beautiful territorial house I have ever seen. They actually put a deposit down with a local builder to construct this house in early 2005, a great time to buy a house they thought.

The house had the most beautiful blonde oak beams inside the house and had a huge great room with 20 foot ceilings...It was really something to behold. This beautiful exterior also came with a two acre lot which could accommodate their pets and any animals they might want to acquire later.

The house was completed in mid 2006. They paid about $650,000. for the home. This was a great price. When they had it appraised to get the purchase loan, there were $700,000 homes in the appraisal with about the same size and amenities. Everything looked good.

When all was said and done, they purchased the home with 20% down (about $130,000.) and got a 1st loan for about $450,000. and a second loan for about $70,000. Based upon what the realtor told them, it would be better to get a first and a second rather than one big purchase loan.

2007, 2008, and 2009 came next. Guess what happened? As some of the homes in their neighborhood were foreclosed upon by their banks, the home values started to drop drastically. One house across from their house sold for $275,000. Although it had only an acre lot and was a bit smaller interior wise, this was very bad for their value and bad for everyone's value in the neighborhood. Then other homes sold in the high 200,000's and low $300,000's.

Now, when all was said and done, their $650,000. home was worth no more than $350,000. That's almost a 50% drop in the property's value. The down payment of $130,000. was now history and was lost. The $520,000. loan was now worth just $350,000. Yet, the monthly mortgage payment on the first loan was $2950. per month.

The mortgage payment on the second loan was also about $450. per month. This meant that their total monthly payment was now $3400. per month for a house that was worth $350,000. at best.

If you are reading this book, perhaps this is familiar to you. Perhaps, way too familiar.

When I spoke to them about this situation, they loved the house. They wanted to stay in the house. Like many other people, however, their income had also been reduced since the "good old days" when they were able to pay $650,000. for the house. They couldn't pay the $3400. per month and were already a couple of payments behind on the 1st and the 2nd.

They asked me what to do. This is what I told them. Seek a HAMP loan modification on the first trust deed for the house. They decided to ignore the 2nd altogether, in the meantime, and try to get a settlement on that loan later for a greatly reduced value since it had no equity.

Let me start with the 2nd first because it is easy to explain.

The 2nd loan for $70,000. did not have any actual equity in it until the property value exceeded $450,000. Since the home was worth no more than $350,000., it had no equity.
As a result, they didn't feel that the lender who made that second loan would foreclose on the home because it wouldn't be getting any value from doing so.

They also considered this question: would the lender sue the owners personally for the loan? They decided that the lender wouldn't do that because they no longer had any money. The owners didn't even have enough money to pay the first and keep their home.

If the owners did have a lot of other money, it is possible that that lender would sue for the amount of its' note. Whether you try to pay your 2nd loan is a personal decision.

They decided to see if the bank sent them a settlement offer for a really reduced amount. I personally think that, in the absence of equity like there was here, that the borrowers could offer 10% or less of the loan (about $7000.) to the lender to pay off the loan in full settlement. The lender might decide to take it at some point.

I do not take any formal position in this book that any valid creditor should not be paid. I do think, however, that a borrower does have to look at how much money he or she has and decide how best to pay it out. This is the decision the above borrowers made, based upon their personal circumstances.

I told them that if they worked out a settlement with the 2nd lender that they should demand that the lender delete all negative credit references relating to this account that they had entered on the credit bureaus and show the mortgage account as "Paid" as a neutral, unrated account so they no longer had any negative credit associated with this mortgage.

So, the decision was made on the 2nd loan: they decided to stop put it on hold until they could actually afford to pay it.

Regarding the 1st loan, we had to deal with that immediately. There was no way around that. Now, typically lenders will file and post on your door a Notice of Default or Notice of Sale (depending upon the state you're in) after about 3 missed payments. That seems to be the magic number of payments to be missed. Up to 3, you're probably OK. After that, start checking your front door and your mail box for bad news about your house.

They were 2 payments behind and, lo and behold, the lender sent them a letter suggesting that they apply for a HAMP loan modification. The loan itself qualified for this program based upon the following:

(1) $729,750. balance or less. (first loan was about $450,000.)
(2) Owner Occupied Home (they lived there!)
(3) Borrowers had financial hardship (they were making substantially less money than during they hey days in the early 2000's and when they took out this loan in

early 2006. (Since the lender was suggesting a HAMP modification, we know that the loan qualified as a Fannie Mae or Freddie Mac loan.)

The question was whether they made enough income to justify the bank agreeing to the modification. Remember, as I said before, you have to show the lender that you make enough money that, after deducting your normal monthly expenses, that you can pay some kind of acceptable mortgage to the bank.

Let me show you what the lender ended up doing and how it compared to the original loan:

I. <u>Original Loan</u>: $450,000. at 5.5% start rate--$2543. per month
Taxes and Insurance: <u>$392</u>. per month.
Total: $2935.

This is the original scheduled mortgage payment for this loan. Please note also that I said "5.5% start rate". That means that the rate was adjustable and it could explode upward big time in the future. That rate increase could be devastating to the family—just like it has been for so many other families around the country.

II. <u>Borrowers' Income</u>: critical toward determining what the lender can/should do.

Now you have to look at the borrowers' income—not just the borrower on the loan, but their spouse also because they both contribute to paying the bills and the mortgage (per the lender).

In this case, the borrower joint income was reduced to roughly $5800. per month.

III. <u>What is 31% of their Gross Income?</u> (gross income—income before taxes deducted; if personal business income then gross receipts less expenses necessary to generate those receipts).

*31% of 5800. per month is $1798. per month. Right off the top, this is the amount of the monthly payment they could receive for the modification—if they found that the borrower could actually afford $1798. per month after perusing their budget.

The bank can also charge the interest rate of 2% to get the payment down to 31% of the borrower's gross income. Here, a 2% rate for $450,000. is a monthly payment of $1660. So, that principle would work.

In our case, the bank looked at the borrower's stated expenses and came to the conclusion that their "gross income" for purposes of their calculation apparently was $4258. per month rather than the $5800. I think that the bank deducted additional tax expense from the application.

This is one of those times that the author cannot specifically explain how the lender came to this calculation. I think that the bank deducted additional tax expense from the application. Or, perhaps the bank didn't want to count the "social security income" from the spouse in the household. which was about $1200. per month.

BUT, once they came to this conclusion, very good things started to happen for this family! Remember when I told you that, with the HAMP Plan, sometimes the bank can give you a modification based upon part of the loan only and put the rest aside?

Well, that happened here. The bank took 31% of what it considered to be the gross income, here $4258., and concluded that a 31% payment would be $1320. per month.

Under the HAMP Plan, the 31% of $1320. per month has to include taxes and insurance.

With those calculations, the actual part of the $1320. per month that went to the mortgage was $985. per month.

How much of a loan balance would this cover? ($985. per month and 2% interest). Further, the bank changed the amortization schedule from 30 to 40 years.

It would cover a loan balance of about $325,000. That means that this lender used the HAMP modification to set up monthly payments for $325,000. with no interest or principal to be paid on the remaining $125,000. of this loan for a minimum of 8 years.

Now, based upon this modification, the new monthly mortgage payment became $1320. per month—including taxes and insurance impounds—while the payment before the modification was $2935. per month. The monthly mortgage was reduced about 55% based upon this modification…what an excellent result!!

This payment was then fixed for 5 full years and there was no negative amortization. In other words, the loan was not getting larger because the interest rate was so low. It was actually getting smaller. The rate would increase slightly, about a percent or two per year, starting in year 6.

The HAMP plan gives the lender a lot of flexibility in terms of how it makes its mods. The bank can basically create a brand new loan at 2% based upon a brand new loan balance which is less, maybe substantially less, than what you started out with. You could start out with a loan of $700,000., payable at 7%, and end up with a new HAMP loan of $500,000., payable at 2%, with the remaining $200,000. put on the backend of the loan. This modification may provide you with an incredible opportunity to keep your home.

Chapter 2: <u>WATCH OUT FOR THIS TYPE OF MODIFICATION SCAM!</u>

While I was living in Phoenix, Arizona, I traveled back to Orange County, California on a regular basis because I was a licensed attorney in California. I had put an ad in Craigslist for loan mod companies that needed an in house counsel.

I received a number of calls on the ad. BUT what these companies, not only in Orange County but in a number of other places, wanted to create was "law firms" where I would be the name of the company.

That sounds nice. The idea of a law firm which brings in thousands of dollars in loan mod dollars sounds sexy, sounds like you'll help a lot of people, and make a lot of money.

That's not the way it was, however. They wanted me as the "attorney" to sign my name to all the loan mod contracts, let them do all the work, and then I would take a specific, agreed amount per file…like $200. per file.

I remember one such company in Irvine, California. These two young dynamos with quite a large building and many people working told me that they were taking in about 300 files per month. At first, they told me that they would set up a "law firm" in my name and that I would receive $75. per file. They would do all the advertising. Also, they would do most of the loan mod work itself. Then I would make about $22,500. per month. These two guys were not attorneys and were not even real estate brokers.

I told them that, in order for there to be a genuine "law firm" that I would have to be in total and actual control of the firm because I was the supervising attorney and that I would have to determine how much I wanted to pay them after I paid myself and my overhead. I also told them that they couldn't be "partners" with me because it is improper for an attorney to be a "partner" in a law firm with a non-attorney.

Once I started to tell them these rules, that was a non-starter fast. We couldn't reach an agreement where there would be a legitimate "law firm" that was being created.

One morning, I remember one of them calling me and saying: "Why don't you come in right now and start taking cases in your name. You can have $200. for each case you get." I told them: "I can't do it that way. I am under certain legal and ethical obligations as a member of the State Bar.

You know what he said to me then? He said: "The Bar will never have to find out about this." I told him: "I can't do it that way." Then he hung up on me never to be heard again. You could tell that he was angry for me taking the approach I did.

It's just this kind of conduct that is the basis for all the loan modification fraud out there. And there's a lot of it!

Many loan mod companies are calling themselves "law firms" or "attorney driven" or "attorney supervised" and there may not even be an attorney actually involved in looking at any of the files. Then you get hurt when you pay them thousands of dollars and don't get any work done on your file.

That's the purpose of this book. Give you some idea of how to do this yourself. Don't get me wrong. There are some honest people out there who know their stuff and will help you with your loan mod, but you better do some research to make sure you decide on the right people.

On another occasion, I had the displeasure of meeting a gentleman who was running another loan mod company in Orange County, California. This is the home of the "bad loans" from the past and the "bad loan mods" of the present.

We actually spoke about the possibility of me setting up a Law Corporation and him and his staff would do my mod processing for me (get the forms filled out, call the lender, call the client for more information).

Ultimately, the new law in California, SB94, was enacted which stated that no loan modification company in California could take money up front from any client and before the loan modification work was completed. At that point, the loan mod business in California was no longer viable, in my opinion. This was due to the fact that many borrowers simply wouldn't pay for their mods after you were completed with the work. So, no more loan mod business.

After I said "no" to working with this guy, I get a call while I'm at Disneyland from a former worker with his company. My wife had taken me to Disneyland for the day for my birthday. My birthday wish every year was for my wife to take me to Disneyland—at least that's the part of my wish that I can tell you about…

This guy had left the company and he told me that the business owner was now operating his business as a "Law Corporation". I asked him: "Who is the supervising attorney?" He told me: "There isn't an attorney. He just calls it a 'Law Corporation.' He said that the business owner said he could get more loan modification business if people thought he was a law firm!

That's really unbelievable—the idea that a person would call his company a "Law Corporation" when he wasn't a Law Corporation, when he could call himself a lawyer when he wasn't a lawyer and wasn't supervised by a lawyer.

I told the former employee to call the District Attorney's Office and immediately report this business owner as engaged in the "unauthorized practice of law" and, further, defrauding the general public by representing that he was a lawyer or engaged in the practice of law when he had no legal credentials whatsoever! This was amazing stuff.

This is the kind of illegal practices that you sometimes run into when talking "loan modification". Many people see this field of endeavor as a means to vast amounts of money without performing the necessary tasks to help people with their loans. That's one of the reasons that California enacted their protective statute SB 94.

I also think that many banks probably "influenced" the California legislature also to change the law and make it impossible to do a loan mod with California citizens. With less professional help, the banks would be freer to do whatever they want to do and provide fewer modifications, even to people who deserved it.

Unfortunately, the California law put the end not only to modification fraud, but to professionally assisted modifications also. Some professional modifications could help a lot of people. That will never happen now because of the degree to which the California legislature acted—to stop bad practices, but also to help the Banks and put them more in control of the entire process!

Chapter 3: <u>I'm Glad Its' You at the Front Door. I didn't want to be served today!</u>

That's something I heard from a friend the other day. You may or may not have encountered this—the tap, tap, tap on your front door—and you're afraid that it might be a process server coming to serve you with a lawsuit. Somebody is suing you to pay them money or suing you to get out of their home (eviction) or suing you for foreclosure (take your home) or suing you for absolutely anything…

In fact, if you have been subject to this, you may have at some point make the decision: "I'm not going to open the door when anyone knocks. I'm going to ask people who have come to see me to call me first and tell me when they are at my front door!" Your world changes when someone sues you, if you're not a very monied person. All of a sudden you're subject to someone else and that person can force you to do anything they want in a court of law if you don't work within the rules of the court and you should probably hire a lawyer to explain to you how to do this.

You understand that when someone gets a judgment against you that they can call you in for an oral examination where they ask you about your assets. They can even try to take away your car or demand that you give them money over and above the state allowed equity exemption for the car. Then you can't go to work or get to the office…

This ties into my discussion of loan modifications.

When I talk about loan modifications, I have to talk about two essentially different types of jurisdictions in this country and how the Courts handle the foreclosures. These are two very different ways of handling the foreclosure and how you have to deal with the process.

First, there is a non-judicial foreclosure type of state such as California or Arizona which **in general,** foreclose on your home by way of a trustee's deed. Here, the bank pretty quickly forecloses on the home without going to Court and without seeking any additional money judgment against you after taking back the home.

Second, there is a judicial foreclosure type of state such as Florida and New Mexico which generally foreclose by virtue of a law suit for foreclosure where the bank (mortgage holder) actually serves you with a summons and complaint (lawsuit) right at your front door and then seeks to foreclose the home, and get a judgment for a cash deficiency against you. That's the difference between the fair market value of the home and the amount of the loan. That can be a lot, especially these days!!

Interestingly enough, the banks in these jurisdictions want to take personal judgments against you even though many of them have been bailed out by the government and even though they get the property back.

Unfortunately, our great congress voted for the bailout of the these lenders but didn't put any condition in the loans that the banks would have to re-lend the money out to worthy buyers, did not establish or define what a "credit worthy" borrower would be, and let the lenders run wild—by getting money judgments from people after foreclosing on their homes. In my opinion, the federal government should have prohibited lenders who took bailout money from filing any deficiency lawsuits against former homeowners after they took their homes away from them!! (both owner occupants and investor home owners).

Please note: this stuff I'm telling you about these states is explained in very general terms. When you're faced with a foreclosure in any of the states mentioned above, I strongly recommend that you meet with a local attorney who is licensed to practice law in the state you find yourself and the property and discuss specific law and specific strategy with him. That's the only way to go.

If you live in a "non-deficiency" state **and** the bank is trying to take back the home through a non-judicial foreclosure, you could come home one day and find a Notice of Default or Notice of Sale or whatever they call the document in your particular state. This means obviously that the Bank is poised and ready to take your home and throw you out on the street after a certain period of time prescribed by state law.

Watch out here: there are some exceptions to the **general idea** that posting of a foreclosure notice on your door means that the bank won't sue you for a deficiency judgment. In the state of Nevada, I've come to learn (from a bankruptcy case I did) that the lender could foreclose from posting a notice of foreclosure on your door (among other things) and could then sue the homeowner personally for a deficiency within a certain period of time. That's a scary twist to this principle. If you live in Nevada, make sure you're aware of the state law regarding how the bank can treat you if they foreclose on your home.

*You should have already applied for a loan modification well before the lender posts any foreclosure notice on your front door. Don't wait to get a foreclosure notice to submit an application to the lender for a loan modification. That's darn ignorant if you do that and can cause you a lot of harm and personal grief.

In fact, I would recommend that you submit a loan modification application to your lender once you know you're in trouble, once you know that your circumstances have changed.

Theoretically, under the HAMP program, you don't have to have missed any mortgage payments to get a loan modification.

In a judicial foreclosure state such as Florida or New Mexico, you will probably get served with a summons and complaint from the bank seeking to foreclose on your home stating also that the bank can seek a money judgment for the "deficiency".

Once you have accepted service of these documents, you will have only so much time to answer or respond according to your local state law. I strongly recommend that you get an attorney to represent you if this happens to you.

In many circumstances, I have found that the Bank's documents are deficient in many respects. They can take an immediate judgment only if you don't answer or respond to their complaint. For instance, I have seen that some of these judicial foreclosure complaints don't properly include the Promissory Note that you allegedly signed when you took out the loan. In many instances, the lenders just type up a piece of paper, type in the terms they believed you agreed to, and attach this as an Exhibit to the foreclosure complaint.

When you answer the complaint, you can very legally and properly deny that this is the Promissory Note. Once you do that, you have delayed the foreclosure proceeding until such time that the Bank can come up with a proper copy of the Promissory Note.

I have also seen instances where the Assignment of the Mortgage is missing. In other words, the bank that is seeking to foreclose on your home can't properly show that it actually owns the note and mortgage upon which it is now suing. You can stop the Bank in its' tracks, at least temporarily, when you deny the authenticity of the included Assignment or assert that it does not exist.

What does this have to do with loan modification, you might ask. Well, by stopping the judicial foreclosure you can get more time to seek a modification with the foreclosing bank. It has been my experience that the "loss mitigation" departments at the bank will continue to process your loan modification even though their hired, independent lawyers are trying to foreclose on your home at the same time.

By delaying the foreclosure lawsuit against you in good faith, you are giving yourself the extra time necessary to seek the modification with the Bank that can help to save your home and cancel the foreclosure. Also, with an agreed modification, you head off the possibility of a deficiency judgment against you for untold thousands of dollars.

Time is important when you are seeking a modification. You need time. You can't get the time to complete an agreement when the bank has your home. Once they get your home, your goose is cooked.

In some instances, you might even gain an advantage with the bank in their foreclosure suit so that you can demand a modification or even a principal reduction. So, never just let a lender serve you without carefully reviewing what they are saying. What they are saying may be incorrect.

Also, I've heard that some authorities on the internet state that banks aren't really pursuing deficiency judgments since they know you don't have any money anyway. This is how I respond to that: the banks can pursue the deficiency judgments for some period of time, depending upon state law. How long does the state law allow the bank to pursue a deficiency judgment on your home? Isn't it possible also that the bank can sell the right to pursue a deficiency judgment against you to a professional collection company for pennies on the dollar and that company can come after you later? Probably "yes".

When that company comes, they may make your life miserable and they will want more than pennies on the dollar because they purchased that note **to make a profit. You're standing in the way between them and the profit they seek. These people are cold hearted. They don't care if they're destroying your life...Just beware of the possibility of deficiency judgments. Take this issue seriously!!**

With a loan modification, you don't get to the point that the bank will take your house and take a judgment against you. The "debt" never gets sold to any nasty third parties and you don't have to worry about hearing from them in the future about paying this mortgage on that home you no longer own.

So, if you are in a "deficiency" jurisdiction or the bank is proceeding against you with a lawsuit to take back your home, there are legal, proper ways to slow down the foreclosure, to oppose the action that they are taking against you, so that you have time to prepare and submit a loan modification to the bank.

This is a different story, however, if you have a second loan on your house. In most instances, if the first is foreclosing on your home and you make a loan mod with that bank, the second obviously remains alive and kicking after the modification.

I spoke about a situation above where the homeowners successfully obtained a wonderful HAMP modification on a home ($2935. down to $1320. per month). In that case, they had a second trust deed that they were not paying. What happens to that loan? It still remains. It is alive. It is just not being paid anything. Since there is no equity in the home, it is unlikely that this loan will foreclose on the home because it has no equity. There is no benefit to foreclosing on the home.

The fact is that these homeowners, like you, if you have a second loan still on the home, will have to take action on this loan at some point. The best way to handle it is to attempt to settle it off at 10% or less at some point in the future when you can afford to do so. That's a generous settlement for a loan that has absolutely no value whatsoever!

Chapter 4: How Does "Short Sale" Figure in to All This?

A "short sale" is another way to get rid of a bad mortgage. It's the counter part to a loan modification. The way that you qualify for the "short sale" also is exactly opposite to the way that you qualify for a loan modification.

Let me show you what I mean.

I talked earlier about how you qualify for a loan modification. You show the bank that, after all your necessary living expenses, that you can qualify for a certain mortgage amount or less.

After revealing your gross income, you deduct all your expenses and taxes to come up with a monthly mortgage figure that you can afford.

Actually, in the budget form, you put in your present mortgage and all your living expenses and taxes and this will show a substantial negative cash flow. Your goal is to have the bank reduce the mortgage to an amount that makes your budget work.

If the bank were to grant you a loan mod, however, this budget, when you put in your new modified mortgage amount, would show a very slight positive cash flow, maybe $50.00.

Obviously, that's the new mortgage amount that you are shooting for, the mortgage amount that you can afford to pay along with all of your other legitimate monthly expenses and taxes and still have a little money left over at the end.

If the lender is willing to grant you the modification you are seeking, you can agree to it and keep the house as long as you are making the payments.

A "short sale" is exactly the opposite to the loan modification in terms of what it takes to qualify.

Now, you are doing a budget for the bank just like you did for the loan modification, BUT you put that great big mortgage into your budget with all your other bills and your entire budget is a mess. There's no way that you can afford this mortgage no matter what the bank does. You are crying "Maya Copa" on this property because this is clearly not a do-able situation.

For example, your monthly mortgage payment is $4000. per month while you have just lost your job. You can tell the lender: "I have just lost my job and I can't afford to make any payment at all!" That's a good one. That's a great hardship! No one can deny that's the best excuse there is not to pay your mortgage.

**When you prepare a financial statement for a bank for a loan modification, include only the expenses that you actually pay. You can list a credit card, for example that you have but tell them: "I don't pay that." This helps the budget. This shows that you have more money to pay the mortgage with them.

**In huge contrast, when you prepare a financial statement for a bank for a short sale, list every credit card and mortgage debt on the sheet that you have and don't refer to the fact that you are paying or not paying in order to show the bank that you are really underwater when it comes to debt.

Remember, you need to show "hardship" whether you're applying for a loan modification or whether you are applying for a "short sale". The hardship in the case of the loan modification means you can still afford a mortgage, but just not as much as you are paying. The hardship in the case of a short sale means that you can't make any reasonable payment for the home on a monthly basis. You definitely need out.

Enclosed you will find attached as Exhibit D a sample hardship letter for a request for short sale. Please note the sharp difference in language between Exhibit C and Exhibit D. In Exhibit C, you want this thing to work. If only the bank could help you a bit with the mortgage, you could keep the property. In Exhibit D, you're done with the property. You just want them to let you sell it and get rid of it.

The loan modification means that you can keep your home, hopefully at terms you can afford. A short sale means that you are selling the home for less than the loan balance with full lender approval and walking away from the home.

So, the package of information you fill out for the lender be it the loan modification or short sale is virtually the same: you have a budget to fill out and a hardship letter.

With the short sale package, however, you must also include a sales contract procured by your local real estate broker or yourself to sell the home to some third party. It's based upon that offer that the lender will determine whether it wants to accept the sales proceeds from that third party to discount their loan, pay it off, and sell the home.

Just a word of caution: it can sometimes take quite a while for a lender to approve a short sale. Assuming the contract is in order, the lender will first order an appraisal of the property to see whether the offer genuinely reflects fair market value for the property.

Each lender is different when it comes to "fair market value". Some lenders may be more lenient and accept a lesser value to get rid of their non-performing loan. Other lenders may be more aggressive and really expect present fair market value. These lenders may give you or your agent a counter offer asking for a higher price in order to agree to sell the home via this sale.

I'm going to share with you a situation that I personally encountered. I had a client with a property in Florida that she had purchased for $325,000. This was a brand new home that had been purchased directly from the lender a couple years back.

When the market turned, its' value dropped fasttttttttt!! By the time I spoke with her, this home was now worth about $150,000.

She signed a listing with a local realtor who procured a sales contract for the home at $140,000. The agent then submitted this offer directly to the lender's loss mitigation dept. to seek approval for the short sale of the home.

In about a month, the lender faxed back a counter offer to the realtor: Sale price of $225,000. Hence, she and her realtor started on the merry-go-round with the lender about the property's value. This counter offer proved that the lender did not know what the property was worth.

So, the realtor had to pull up every sale of comparable homes in the local area and send them to the lender to change the lender's mind. She had already told the lender that the counter of $225,000. was way above the market value. There was no way that the buyer would sign that deal. Also, there was no way that the buyer could ever get a purchase loan for that price because he could never get it appraised by any other lender for that high value.

After sending letter and sales comps to the lender, the lender finally agreed to accept the offer at the $140,000. price. This was about two months after the offer was first submitted by the buyer. At just about the time the lender accepted the lower offer, the buyer pulled out of the deal and said he didn't want to buy the house anymore…The whole thing was just taking way too long…

So, as you can see, two of the biggest problems with these short sales is (1) getting the lender to be realistic on value and (2) time—how long it takes the lender to get it together and accept the offer.

Then once these two conditions are satisfied, the buyer himself must still qualify for a new purchase loan from another bank—unless he is paying all cash and obtaining no financing.

Then, finally on closing day, you will receive an Agreement from the bank. You are hoping that it says that you have received a "full release" of liability from that loan. If so, that's great. You can walk way and not be concerned any further about that first loan. If not, if this agreement states that you remain liable for any deficiency, this is not a good agreement for you. You need to get back to the drawing board and demand or have your realtor or attorney demand that the bank take the proceeds from the buyer in "full payment" of the loan.

Here's another potential challenge. If the home has a second loan, this can be a real complication to getting the short sale done. The lender in second position typically is asked to take, maybe $2000. or $3000. for its' entire loan in order to release its' lien on the home. So, a lender with a $35,000. loan may be asked to take $2000. in full settlement. Not to worry- the first lender will typically pay this amount to the second lender to pay off the note. The homeowner is not typically asked to do this.

Many lenders will accept this much lower amount because they know that you're not good for it and because they know that the property is certainly not good for it anymore either. The lender realizes that, if it foreclosed on the home, it would get absolutely nothing at all. There would be no equity to pay off any of the value of its note. Also, they know that you would probably file bankruptcy if they pursued you.

The two primary concerns for you here are: (1) value of the property and (2) getting a full release of liability on this second loan. We see this second issue again.

These second lenders want proof that their loan has no equity because the value of the property is very low. Your realtor must prove this to them in order for them to take the major haircut that you're asking them to take with that loan.
Next, and I have seen this, the lender may say that they will accept the lower amount of cash offered by the first lender so that the property will be sold BUT you will remain liable on the second note as a *personal obligation (like I already discussed above with the 1st loan.)*

Sometimes the second loan is really bluffing you when they say this. Sometimes they aren't. Let me give you two contrasting examples.

In one case, I had a client with a home in Arizona that he wanted to get rid of via a short sale. In fact, he had sold the home to his tenants who were living in the home. The loan amount for the first loan was $280,000. and the second loan amount was $28,000. The final agreed sales price was $230,000.

The first lender agreed to the price of $230,000., a complete release of liability to my client for the balance of the loan. As part of this deal, the first loan holder agreed to pay to the 2nd loan holder the amount of $2500.

When the 2nd loan sent the release form over to my client, it said that the bank would accept the $2500. to release its' lien from the house so that the sale could be completed. My client, however, would remain liable and responsible for the balance of the loan even after the home was sold.

He asked me what I thought about that. I told him that that was "whac". I told him to go back to the 2nd lender and say that he wouldn't accept it unless the payment of $2500. was deemed a "full and complete" payoff of the loan and that he would not longer be responsible for anything on the loan.

Actually, I suggested that he take the original release form from the bank and put a big X through it and tell them exactly what I said above. In about 45 minutes, the bank agent called and said that they sent him the "wrong form" and would send a new form showing a complete payoff. The new form was sent to the client later in the afternoon and the whole deal was done—no more liability on that second and the house was sold.

In sharp contrast, a client of mine has a property in Florida where the 2nd lender sent the same kind of release form over to my client: they'd accept the $4000. from the 1st but the client would remain responsible for the balance of the loan. In that case, the lender held firm to that. It would never change that. My client would not agree to remain liable on the 2nd and the whole deal fell through. What a stupid thing for that 2nd lender to do!! It never got anything for that loan…

Also, its' important to mention that the second loan holder often is just not cooperative about any of the short sale stuff you're doing. That bank can just refuse to take what is being offered by the first lender. It can demand more money. It can do absolutely anything it wants to do. A short sale with a second trust deed lender involved is a much more involved, tricky process than where there is only one lender involved, no doubt.

Chapter 5: <u>WHAT IS A "DEED IN LIEU OF FORECLOSURE"?</u>

A "deed in lieu of foreclosure" is another way to get rid of a bad mortgage for you. This is where the lender agrees to take back the home without a foreclosure and you agree to deed the home directly back to the lender. The reason that you would do this is because you want to avoid a foreclosure on your credit report and, in judicial foreclosure states, you're hoping that the lender will agree to take no deficiency judgment from you when they take the deed in lieu of foreclosure.

Now, I'll speak about this device more specifically. Typically, before the lender will consider taking a "deed in lieu", it would like to see that you first tried to sell the house on the open market for a fair market value. It would like to see that, although you did try to sell the house for at least 60 days, you couldn't get a willing and able buyer. As a result, you're now stuck with the mortgage and you really can't do anything about it.

The lender's first preference is always a "short sale" before considering a "deed in lieu". That's because the lender gets the house sold in a short sale and gets cash for its' mortgage. The lender doesn't take the property back in a foreclosure sale and have to keep and manage and list the property for sale through a realtor or REO dept. The property is gone through a short sale and, so, the lender doesn't have to worry about it anymore.

A "deed in lieu", however, is a different animal. Here, the lender is agreeing to take the home back directly from the borrower. The lender will have to take ownership of the home. It will have to manage it and repair it and do something with it. Since lenders don't want to own residential properties, it will probably have to list it for sale and be responsible for it until it is sold to some third party purchaser. This is not a preferred choice for the lender.

But, if it appears that the home or property can't be sold on the regular market and the borrower is definitely not good to make up any deficiency (if a deficiency state or in a state where the bank has the right to seek a deficiency against you), the lender may actually save some costs of foreclosure if it cuts to the chase and just takes back the property directly. And you and the lender are all done.

This is one thing to be aware of. Lenders will generally <u>not</u> give you or any borrower a "deed in lieu" on a first loan if you have a second loan on the property. The first loan must be by itself. If you have a second loan on the property, its' best to try to settle out the second loan by yourself (offer a small amount…5-10% of balance) and then seek a deed in lieu of foreclosure on the first loan—once the second is settled out.

Here's an example of where a "deed in lieu" worked. A client of mine owned a beautiful home in Florida which she purchased for $359,000. When she bought the home in 2006, she put 20% down and took out a loan for about $280,000. There was no second loan on the home.

Within the next few years, the value plummeted to under $200,000. She listed it with an excellent local realtor who brought in offer after offer which the lender would not accept. The lender kept countering at much higher prices that didn't reflect present market conditions.

Once it became apparent that the lender wouldn't accept offers to sell the home and 3 months had elapsed on the listing, she requested that the bank accept a "deed in lieu of foreclosure" on the home. Here, it seemed like the conditions were perfect for getting a deed from the bank: (1) property marketed for sale for considerable time with no acceptable offers; (2) no second trust deed, and (3) "hardship" seller/borrower.

When considering whether or not to agree to a deed in lieu of foreclosure, the bank looks at the very same hardship application that you filed to get approved to do a short sale. They review all the very same documents. You usually don't have to refile any kind of a new application, although it is possible that the bank may request an update on some documents such as bank statements, etc.

In the case of my client, the bank fairly quickly approved the deed in lieu of foreclosure. The bank informed her that it was instructing its' foreclosure attorney in Florida to prepare the necessary documents. Well, that was a real stopper. The firm which this bank had hired to do its' foreclosures in Florida took months to do anything—it was really equipped only to do default foreclosures, not really equipped to do settlements of any kind or actually write custom letters and custom agreements or talk to borrowers or anything of the sort. This law firm was a "foreclosure mill."

It took about six months from the time the bank first told her that it was agreeing to a deed in lieu of foreclosure to the date that the deed actually arrived from the bank's law firm. Oh, what a relief! But what a time delay!! It wasn't that the bank was deliberating on its' decision whether or not to do a deed in lieu of foreclosure. It was merely that the bank's foreclosure firm really wasn't set up or equipped to do any sort of custom work. These foreclosure mills, and there are many of them around the country, merely process standard paperwork over and over to foreclose on homes. They get paid presumably per foreclosure. So, everything else must seem like a real distraction to them!

When she received the Deed agreement from the bank, it stated that there would be no deficiency judgment possible (yahh!!) and that the value of the property at the time of this agreement would be the same price that she (the borrower) paid for the property. This was excellent because there wouldn't be substantial tax consequences through the issuance of a 1099 for "income forgiveness" which could be deemed "ordinary income" by the IRS for tax purposes.

I'm not a CPA and am not seeking to give you accountancy advice through this publication. You do have to be aware, however, that loan mods, foreclosures short sales, and deeds in lieu of foreclosure can have tax consequences for you. You should confer with a professional in the tax field before deciding to proceed with any of these concepts.

A couple years back, new legislation was passed by the federal gov't regarding tax losses on your own personal residence if you have a distress situation. This helped to reduce your tax liability in these situations. You should review this law or have your tax professional review this law if you are selling your own personal residence.

One thing, again, that makes this an easier type of transaction is that there is no second lender to fool with—as I've discussed above with short sales. Since there is just one decision maker, there is one decision and you don't have to dance around the second loan holder.

CONCLUSION: <u>Look at Your Overall Picture</u>!

First, ask yourself: what do I seek to accomplish here? Do I want to keep the home or do I want to sell it?

Remember: don't make the fact that you are in a negative equity position in your home ("underwater") determine the answer to your question.

You may be "underwater" but maintain a great personal lifestyle in that home. You can paint the home; you can do whatever you want to that home because you own it. You can have your dogs and cats and bunny rabbits and you're not subject to anyone's approval or disapproval. Also, you may feel good being in your own home.

In contrast, how will you feel if you lose your home? Will that put a cloud over the rest of your life so that you cannot move forward emotionally and psychologically in a positive way? How will a foreclosure or "deed in lieu" impact your spouse and your children or other family members? Will you lose your piece of mind because you merely give up your home?

These are the base emotional questions you must ask yourself.

Next, what would it cost you to rent an equivalent property? If the loan mod offered is much higher than this, you must balance out whether there is sufficient advantage to stay in your home with the lower cost of the rental substitute vs. the lifestyle you gain from being in your own home.

If the loan mod offered is about the same or less than an equivalent rental, you should definitely consider staying in the home because: "what's the downside to owning your own home with lifestyle included where the cost of an equivalent rental is basically the same or more?

*Also, remember when you own your own home, you can take the home mortgage interest as a tax deduction. You cannot typically deduct your rental payments.

I've heard people talk about the fact that they're walking away from their home merely because they are "underwater" on the mortgage balance in relation to current value. Frankly, in my personal opinion, "equity" is irrelevant right now. Lifestyle, comfort, security, and happiness should come first—that doesn't include walking away from your home if you are offered a good loan mod or might be able to get one. The HAMP program offers you that possibility.

If you are suffering from some terrible hardship and you cannot keep your home, consider the other vehicles to get rid of your bad mortgage.

Try the "short sale". If you have a 1st loan only and you can't get a short sale offer in front of the bank within a reasonable time (60-90 days), try the "deed in lieu" vehicle.

In either case, however, be vigilant of what the final agreement with the bank says: make sure that it says and means that you will be *completely released* from any further liability on that loan. It would be a great idea to retain a local attorney just to review any agreements that come from a 1st or 2nd lender so that you get the complete sign off of liability that you are seeking here.

I wish you the very best with your home and hope that these materials give you some insight how to better and more easily deal with the home mortgage you have at this time.
END

EXHIBIT "A"

3417 COLLEGE PARK • P.O. BOX 1706 • SCOTTSBLUFF, NE 69363-1706
PHONE: 800-550-0509 • FAX: 310-728-7488

Home Affordable Modification Program (HAMP)

Depending upon your current financial situation, it may be possible for Aurora Loan Services LLC (Aurora Loan Services) to offer you a loan modification under the Home Affordable Modification Program (HAMP). HAMP is a loan modification program sponsored by the federal government as part of President Obama's Homeowner Affordability and Stability Plan and the Making Home Affordable Plan. This program may allow us to modify one or more of your original mortgage terms (such as reducing your interest rate or extending your loan term) to provide you with a more affordable payment. A HAMP modification of your mortgage terms may help you avoid foreclosure. **If your loan is insured by the Federal Housing Agency or guaranteed by the Veterans Administration, please refer to the FHA Option web page and the VA Option web page details available on myauroraloan.com.**

You may be eligible for a HAMP modification if you are delinquent or are in imminent danger of becoming delinquent on your mortgage loan account **and** if you occupy the subject property as your primary residence. To begin assessing your potential eligibility for HAMP, you may:

- ✓ log into your mortgage loan account at www.myauroraloan.com as we have posted a notation regarding your potential HAMP eligibility; or
- ✓ review our self-assessment tools; or
- ✓ call us toll free at 1-800-550-0509 and ask to speak with a Foreclosure Prevention Specialists regarding HAMP eligibility

---

If you would like to be considered for a HAMP loan modification transaction, you will need to submit the following financial information and documentation to Aurora Loan Services. *All of the required financial information and documentation must be received by Aurora Loan Services before a full evaluation of your request for a HAMP modification can be made.*

Financial Information and Documentation Requirements

- ☐ A fully completed and signed (by all borrowers) MHA Request for Modification & Affidavit (RMA) and addendum
- ☐ A signed and dated copy of IRS Form 4506-T (**Request for Transcript of Tax Return**) for each borrower. Borrowers who filed their tax returns jointly may provide one IRS Form 4506-T signed and dated by all of the joint filers
- ☐ A copy of the most recently filed **signed** **federal tax return** with all schedules, including Schedule E-Supplemental Income and Loss and Schedule C-Profit and Loss from Business for all borrowers
  - → Note: For borrowers with rental properties, only 75% of the gross rents minus applicable monthly housing payments will be used for qualifying income under HAMP
- ☐ For each borrower who receives a **salary or hourly wages,** copies of that borrower's two most recent pay stubs that show year-to-date earnings
- ☐ For each borrower who is **self-employed,** a copy that borrower's most recent quarterly or year-to-date profit/loss statement
- ☐ For each borrower who has income such as **social security, disability or death benefits, pension, adoption assistance, public assistance, or unemployment:**
  - → A copy of the benefits statement or letter from the provider that states the amount and frequency of payments, and
  - → Copies of the two most recent bank statements showing receipt of such payments.

  Note: If you are unemployed, please refer to the Home Affordable Unemployment Plan details before submitting a request for a HAMP modification. You may be eligible for a temporary forbearance plan. For HAMP, depending on the owner/investor for your loan, we may not be able to use unemployment income as qualifying income. If we are able to use your unemployment income, it must continue for at least 9 months to be considered qualifying income under HAMP.

- ☐ For each borrower who is relying on **alimony, child support or separation maintenance** as qualifying income*
  - → A copy of the divorce decree, separation agreement, other written agreement filed with the court that states the amount and frequency of payments, and
  - → Copies of the two most recent bank statements showing receipt of such payments.

  *You are not required to disclose child support, alimony or separation maintenance income, unless you choose to have it considered in support of your request for a possible HAMP modification

Equal Housing Lender

5417 COLLEGE PARK • PO. BOX 1706 • SCOTTSBLUFF, NE 69363-1706
PHONE 800-550-0509 • FAX 800-278-4038

☐ For each borrower who has **non-wage income (part time employment, bonuses, tips and investment income)**, a copy of the documentation describing the nature of the income (e.g., an employment contract or printouts documenting tip income)

Financial Information and Documentation may be sent:
- ✓ Via fax at 1-866-517-7975, ATTN: Loss Mitigation; or
- ✓ Via mail to one of the following addresses:

Overnight Delivery Services:	U. S. Postal Services:
Aurora Loan Services	Aurora Loan Services
Attention: Loss Mitigation	Attention: Loss Mitigation
2617 College Park	PO Box 1706
Scottsbluff, NE 69361	Scottsbluff, NE 69363-1706

Upon receipt and review of all of the requested financial information and documentation, we will advise you of our decision. **We will not be able to process your request without all of the financial information and documentation requested above, as well as complete and accurate financial information. If you submit an incomplete package to us, it can significantly lengthen the time it will take us to finish our review.**

Please note the following:
- ✓ Prior to modifying your loan, Aurora Loan Services will review the documentation that you provide to determine your eligibility
- ✓ You must complete a HAMP trial period repayment plan
- ✓ Unless otherwise prohibited by state regulations, you will be required to establish an escrow account for the payment of taxes and insurance
- ✓ With our approval it is possible to add another individual to your loan obligation
- ✓ You may be required to attend Housing Counseling provided by a HUD-certified Counselor
- ✓ Additional documentation may be required

Important Additional Information
It is important to understand that contacting our office will not suspend your obligation to make your mortgage loan payments. Aurora Loan Services will continue with collection activities, which may include referring your account for foreclosure, until such time as Aurora Loan Services has approved your request for a HAMP modification.

See attached Important Notice document.

We look forward to working with you. If you have any questions, please call one of our Foreclosure Prevention Specialists toll free at 1-800-550-0509. Additional assistance is available by calling the HOPE Hotline Number toll free at 1-888-995-HOPE and request Making Home Affordable Help. The HOPE Hotline is available free of charge and will connect you with a HUD-certified housing counselor.

Warning Concerning Foreclosure Rescue Scams: You should be careful of people who approach you with offers to "save" your home. You should be extremely careful about any such promises and any suggestions that you pay them a fee or sign over your property to them. State law may require anyone offering such services for profit to enter into a contract which fully describes the services they will perform and fees they will charge you, and may prohibit them from taking any money from you until they have completed all such promised services.

Aurora Loan Services is a debt collector. Aurora Loan Services is attempting to collect a debt and any information obtained will be used for that purpose. However, if you are in bankruptcy or received a bankruptcy discharge of this debt, this communication is not an attempt to collect the debt against you personally, but is notice of a possible enforcement of the lien against the collateral property.

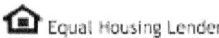 Equal Housing Lender

Aurora • Loan Services

4637 COLLEGE PARK • P.O. BOX 1706 • SCOTTSBLUFF, NE 69363-1706
PHONE 800 550-0508 • FAX 866-228-2606

IMPORTANT NOTICE

If a duly-noticed foreclosure sale has been scheduled, any approval of a foreclosure alternative option is contingent upon the ability of Aurora Loan Services LLC (Aurora Loan Services) to have the pending foreclosure sale postponed or cancelled.

Aurora Loan Services is a debt collector. Aurora Loan Services is attempting to collect a debt and any information obtained will be used for that purpose. However, if you are in bankruptcy or received a bankruptcy discharge of this debt, this communication is not an attempt to collect the debt against you personally, but is notice of a possible enforcement of the lien against the collateral property.

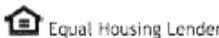 Equal Housing Lender

Making Home Affordable Program
Request For Modification and Affidavit (RMA)

MAKING HOME AFFORDABLE.gov

▶ Loan I.D. Number _____   ▶ Servicer _____

BORROWER	CO-BORROWER
Borrower's name	Co-borrower's name
Social Security number Date of birth	Social Security number Date of birth
Home phone number with area code	Home phone number with area code
Cell or work number with area code	Cell or work number with area code

I want to:	Keep the Property	Sell the Property
The property is my:	Primary Residence	Second Home Investment
The property is:	Owner Occupied	Renter Occupied Vacant

Mailing address

Property address (if same as mailing address, just write same)   E-mail address

Is the property listed for sale?   Yes   No
Have you received an offer on the property?   Yes   No
Date of offer _____ Amount of offer $ _____
Agent's Name: _____
Agent's Phone Number: _____
For Sale by Owner?   Yes   No

Have you contacted a credit-counseling agency for help   Yes   No
If yes, please complete the following:
Counselor's Name: _____
Agency Name: _____
Counselor's Phone Number: _____
Counselor's E-mail: _____

Who pays the real estate tax bill on your property?
   I do   Lender does   Paid by condo or HOA
Are the taxes current?   Yes   No
Condominium or HOA Fees   Yes   No $ _____
Paid to: _____

Who pays the hazard insurance premium for your property?
   I do   Lender does   Paid by Condo or HOA
Is the policy current?   Yes   No
Name of Insurance Co.: _____
Insurance Co. Tel #: _____

Have you filed for bankruptcy?   Yes   No   If yes.   Chapter 7   Chapter 13   Filing Date: _____
Has your bankruptcy been discharged?   Yes   No   Bankruptcy case number _____

Additional Liens/Mortgages or Judgments on this property:

Lien Holder's Name/Servicer	Balance	Contact Number	Loan Number

HARDSHIP AFFIDAVIT

I (We) am/are requesting review under the Making Home Affordable program.
I am having difficulty making my monthly payment because of financial difficulties created by (check all that apply):

My household income has been reduced. For example: unemployment, underemployment, reduced pay or hours, decline in business earnings, death, disability or divorce of a borrower or co-borrower.

My monthly debt payments are excessive and I am overextended with my creditors. Debt includes credit cards, home equity or other debt.

My expenses have increased. For example: monthly mortgage payment reset, high medical or health care costs, uninsured losses, increased utilities or property taxes.

My cash reserves, including all liquid assets, are insufficient to maintain my current mortgage payment and cover basic living expenses at the same time.

Other.

Explanation (continue on back of page 3 if necessary). _____
_____

page 1 of 3 ▶

INCOME/EXPENSES FOR HOUSEHOLD[1]

Number of People in Household:

Monthly Household Income		Monthly Household Expenses/Debt		Household Assets	
Monthly Gross Wages	$	First Mortgage Payment	$	Checking Account(s)	$
Overtime	$	Second Mortgage Payment	$	Checking Account(s)	$
Child Support / Alimony / Separation[2]	$	Insurance	$	Savings/ Money Market	$
Social Security/SSDI	$	Property Taxes	$	CDs	$
Other monthly income from pensions, annuities or retirement plans	$	Credit Cards / Installment Loan(s) (total minimum payment per month)	$	Stocks / Bonds	$
Tips, commissions, bonus and self-employed income	$	Alimony, child support payments	$	Other Cash on Hand	$
Rents Received	$	Net Rental Expenses	$	Other Real Estate (estimated value)	$
Unemployment Income	$	HOA/Condo Fees/Property Maintenance	$	Other _____	$
Food Stamps/Welfare	$	Car Payments	$	Other _____	$
Other (investment income, royalties, interest, dividends etc.)	$	Other _____ _____	$	Do not include the value of life insurance or retirement plans when calculating assets (401 k, pension funds, annuities, IRAs, Keogh plans, etc.)	
Total (Gross Income)	**$**	**Total Debt/Expenses**	**$**	**Total Assets**	**$**

INCOME MUST BE DOCUMENTED

[1]Include combined income and expenses from the borrower and co-borrower (if any). If you include income and expenses from a household member who is not a borrower, please specify using the back of this form if necessary.

[2]You are not required to disclose Child Support, Alimony or Separation Maintenance Income, unless you choose to have it considered by your servicer.

INFORMATION FOR GOVERNMENT MONITORING PURPOSES

The following information is requested by the federal government in order to monitor compliance with federal statutes that prohibit discrimination in housing. **You are not required to furnish this information, but are encouraged to do so. The law provides that a lender or servicer may not discriminate either on the basis of this information, or on whether you choose to furnish it.** If you furnish the information, please provide both ethnicity and race. For race, you may check more than one designation. If you do not furnish ethnicity, race, or sex, the lender or servicer is required to note the information on the basis of visual observation or surname if you have made this request for a loan modification in person. **If you do not wish to furnish the information, please check the box below.**

BORROWER	☐ I do not wish to furnish this information	CO-BORROWER	☐ I do not wish to furnish this information
Ethnicity:	Hispanic or Latino Not Hispanic or Latino	Ethnicity:	Hispanic or Latino Not Hispanic or Latino
Race:	American Indian or Alaska Native Asian Black or African American Native Hawaiian or Other Pacific Islander White	Race:	American Indian or Alaska Native Asian Black or African American Native Hawaiian or Other Pacific Islander White
Sex:	Female Male	Sex:	Female Male

To be completed by interviewer

Name/Address of Interviewer's Employer

This request was taken by:	Interviewer's Name (print or type) & ID Number
Face-to-face interview Mail	Interviewer's Signature Date
Telephone Internet	Interviewer's Phone Number (include area code)

ACKNOWLEDGEMENT AND AGREEMENT

In making this request for consideration under the Making Home Affordable Program, I certify under penalty of perjury:

1. That all of the information in this document is truthful and the event(s) identified on page 1 is/are the reason that need to request a modification of the terms of my mortgage loan, short sale or deed-in-lieu of foreclosure.

2. I understand that the Servicer, the U.S. Department of the Treasury, or their agents may investigate the accuracy of my statements and may require me to provide supporting documentation. I also understand that knowingly submitting false information may violate Federal law.

3. I understand the Servicer will pull a current credit report on all borrowers obligated on the Note.

4. I understand that if I have intentionally defaulted on my existing mortgage, engaged in fraud or misrepresented any fact(s) in connection with this document, the Servicer may cancel any Agreement under Making Home Affordable and may pursue foreclosure on my home.

5. That: my property is owner-occupied; I intend to reside in this property for the next twelve months; I have not received a condemnation notice; and there has been no change in the ownership of the Property since I signed the documents for the mortgage that I want to modify.

6. I am willing to provide all requested documents and to respond to all Servicer questions in a timely manner.

7. I understand that the Servicer will use the information in this document to evaluate my eligibility for a loan modification or short sale or deed-in-lieu of foreclosure, but the Servicer is not obligated to offer me assistance based solely on the statements in this document.

8. I am willing to commit to credit counseling if it is determined that my financial hardship is related to excessive debt.

9. I understand that the Servicer will collect and record personal information, including, but not limited to, my name, address, telephone number, social security number, credit score, income, payment history, government monitoring information, and information about account balances and activity. I understand and consent to the disclosure of my personal information and the terms of any Making Home Affordable Agreement by Servicer to (a) the U.S. Department of the Treasury, (b) Fannie Mae and Freddie Mac in connection with their responsibilities under the Homeowner Affordability and Stability Plan; (c) any investor, insurer, guarantor or servicer that owns, insures, guarantees or services my first lien or subordinate lien (if applicable) mortgage loan(s); (d) companies that perform support services in conjunction with Making Home Affordable; and (e) any HUD-certified housing counselor.

▶ _____   _____

Borrower Signature   Date

▶ _____   _____

Co-Borrower Signature   Date

5417 COLLEGE PARK · P.O. BOX 1706 · SCOTTSBLUFF, NE 69363-1706
PHONE 800-550-0508 · FAX 310-728-2008

Making Home Affordable Program
Request for Modification and Affidavit
Addendum

Borrower Name(s): _____

Loan #: _____

Property Address: _____

Servicer: Aurora Loan Services LLC

If you have reported an amount in the 'Other' box on page 2 of the Request for Modification and Affidavit (RMA) under the Monthly Household Expenses/Debt column, please complete the table below to provide a breakdown of the expenses/debt provided in the 'Other' box. This itemization is necessary to ensure all appropriate expenses and debts are considered in our review of your HAMP Loan Modification request.

Itemization of 'other' Monthly Household Expenses/Debt	Monthly Amount
Food	$
Utilities (electric, gas, telephone, cell phone, etc.)	$
Transportation	$
Cable/internet	$
Medical bills/Co-pay	$
Insurance premiums (life, auto, etc.)	$
Any additional property maintenance costs	$
All non-HOA property dues or maintenance fees	
Other:	$
Other:	$
Other:	$
Total Other Expenses*	

* This total must match the amount in the 'Other' box on page 2 of the RMA under the Monthly Household Expenses/Debt column.

Signed:

_____   _____
Borrower   Date

_____   _____
Borrower   Date

_____   _____
Borrower   Date

_____   _____
Borrower   Date

Equal Housing Lender

Form **4506-T**

(Rev. January 2010)

Department of the Treasury
Internal Revenue Service

Request for Transcript of Tax Return

▶ Request may be rejected if the form is incomplete or illegible.

OMB No. 1545-1872

Tip. Use Form 4506-T to order a transcript or other return information free of charge. See the product list below. You can also call 1-800-829-1040 to order a transcript. If you need a copy of your return, use **Form 4506, Request for Copy of Tax Return.** There is a fee to get a copy of your return.

1a Name shown on tax return. If a joint return, enter the name shown first.	1b First social security number on tax return or employer identification number (see instructions)
2a If a joint return, enter spouse's name shown on tax return	2b Second social security number if joint tax return

3   Current name, address (including apt., room, or suite no.), city, state, and ZIP code

4   Previous address shown on the last return filed if different from line 3

5   If the transcript or tax information is to be mailed to a third party (such as a mortgage company), enter the third party's name, address, and telephone number. The IRS has no control over what the third party does with the tax information.

Caution. *If the transcript is being mailed to a third party, ensure that you have filled in line 6 and line 9 before signing. Sign and date the form once you have filled in these lines. Completing these steps helps to protect your privacy.*

6   **Transcript requested.** Enter the tax form number here (1040, 1065, 1120, etc.) and check the appropriate box below. Enter only one tax form number per request. ▶

a   **Return Transcript,** which includes most of the line items of a tax return as filed with the IRS. A tax return transcript does not reflect changes made to the account after the return is processed. Transcripts are only available for the following returns: Form 1040 series, Form 1065, Form 1120, Form 1120A, Form 1120H, Form 1120L, and Form 1120S. Return transcripts are available for the current year and returns processed during the prior 3 processing years. Most requests will be processed within 10 business days ☐

b   **Account Transcript,** which contains information on the financial status of the account, such as payments made on the account, penalty assessments, and adjustments made by you or the IRS after the return was filed. Return information is limited to items such as tax liability and estimated tax payments. Account transcripts are available for most returns. Most requests will be processed within 30 calendar days ☐

c   **Record of Account,** which is a combination of line item information and later adjustments to the account. Available for current year and 3 prior tax years. Most requests will be processed within 30 calendar days ☐

7   **Verification of Nonfiling,** which is proof from the IRS that you **did not** file a return for the year. Current year requests are only available after June 15th. There are no availability restrictions on prior year requests. Most requests will be processed within 10 business days ☐

8   **Form W-2, Form 1099 series, Form 1098 series, or Form 5498 series transcript.** The IRS can provide a transcript that includes data from these information returns. State or local information is not included with the Form W-2 information. The IRS may be able to provide this transcript information for up to 10 years. Information for the current year is generally not available until the year after it is filed with the IRS. For example, W-2 information for 2007, filed in 2008, will not be available from the IRS until 2009. If you need W-2 information for retirement purposes, you should contact the Social Security Administration at 1-800-772-1213. Most requests will be processed within 45 days ☐

Caution. *If you need a copy of Form W-2 or Form 1099, you should first contact the payer. To get a copy of the Form W-2 or Form 1099 filed with your return, you must use Form 4506 and request a copy of your return, which includes all attachments.*

9   **Year or period requested.** Enter the ending date of the year or period, using the mm/dd/yyyy format. If you are requesting more than four years or periods, you must attach another Form 4506-T. For requests relating to quarterly tax returns, such as Form 941, you must enter each quarter or tax period separately.

Signature of taxpayer(s). I declare that I am either the taxpayer whose name is shown on line 1a or 2a, or a person authorized to obtain the tax information requested. If the request applies to a joint return, **either** husband or wife must sign. If signed by a corporate officer, partner, guardian, tax matters partner, executor, receiver, administrator, trustee, or party other than the taxpayer, I certify that I have the authority to execute Form 4506-T on behalf of the taxpayer. **Note.** *For transcripts being sent to a third party, this form must be received within 120 days of signature date.*

Telephone number of taxpayer on line 1a or 2a

Sign Here	▶ Signature (see instructions)	Date
	▶ Title (if line 1a above is a corporation, partnership, estate, or trust)	
	▶ Spouse's signature	Date

For Privacy Act and Paperwork Reduction Act Notice, see page 2.

Cat. No. 37667N

Form **4506-T** (Rev. 1-2010)

General Instructions

Purpose of form. Use Form 4506-T to request tax return information. You can also designate a third party to receive the information. See line 5.

Tip. Use Form 4506, Request for Copy of Tax Return, to request copies of tax returns.

Where to file. Mail or fax Form 4506-T to the address below for the state you lived in, or the state your business was in, when that return was filed. There are two address charts: one for individual transcripts (Form 1040 series and Form W-2) and one for all other transcripts.

If you are requesting more than one transcript or other product and the chart below shows two different RAIVS teams, send your request to the team based on the address of your most recent return.

Automated transcript request. You can call 1-800-829-1040 to order a transcript through the automated self-help system. Follow prompts for "questions about your tax account" to order a tax return transcript.

Chart for individual transcripts (Form 1040 series and Form W-2)

If you filed an individual return and lived in:	Mail or fax to the "Internal Revenue Service" at:
Florida, Georgia, North Carolina, South Carolina	RAIVS Team P.O. Box 47-421 Stop 91 Doraville, GA 30362 770-455-2335
Alabama, Kentucky, Louisiana, Mississippi, Tennessee, Texas, a foreign country, or A.P.O. or F.P.O. address	RAIVS Team Stop 6716 AUSC Austin, TX 73301 512-460-2272
Alaska, Arizona, California, Colorado, Hawaii, Idaho, Illinois, Indiana, Iowa, Kansas, Michigan, Minnesota, Montana, Nebraska, Nevada, New Mexico, North Dakota, Oklahoma, Oregon, South Dakota, Utah, Washington, Wisconsin, Wyoming	RAIVS Team Stop 37106 Fresno, CA 93888 559-456-5876
Arkansas, Connecticut, Delaware, District of Columbia, Maine, Maryland, Massachusetts, Missouri, New Hampshire, New Jersey, New York, Ohio, Pennsylvania, Rhode Island, Vermont, Virginia, West Virginia	RAIVS Team Stop 6705 P-6 Kansas City, MO 64999 816-292-6102

Chart for all other transcripts

If you lived in or your business was in:	Mail or fax to the "Internal Revenue Service" at:
Alabama, Alaska, Arizona, Arkansas, California, Colorado, Florida, Hawaii, Idaho, Iowa, Kansas, Louisiana, Minnesota, Mississippi, Missouri, Montana, Nebraska, Nevada, New Mexico, North Dakota, Oklahoma, Oregon, South Dakota, Tennessee, Texas, Utah, Washington, Wyoming, a foreign country, or A.P.O. or F.P.O. address	RAIVS Team P.O. Box 9941 Mail Stop 6734 Ogden, UT 84409 801-620-6922
Connecticut, Delaware, District of Columbia, Georgia, Illinois, Indiana, Kentucky, Maine, Maryland, Massachusetts, Michigan, New Hampshire, New Jersey, New York, North Carolina, Ohio, Pennsylvania, Rhode Island, South Carolina, Vermont, Virginia, West Virginia, Wisconsin	RAIVS Team P.O. Box 145500 Stop 2800 F Cincinnati, OH 45250 859-669-3592

Line 1b. Enter your employer identification number (EIN) if your request relates to a business return. Otherwise, enter the first social security number (SSN) shown on the return. For example, if you are requesting Form 1040 that includes Schedule C (Form 1040), enter your SSN.

Line 6. Enter only one tax form number per request.

Signature and date. Form 4506-T must be signed and dated by the taxpayer listed on line 1a or 2a. If you completed line 5 requesting the information be sent to a third party, the IRS must receive Form 4506-T within 120 days of the date signed by the taxpayer or it will be rejected.

Individuals. Transcripts of jointly filed tax returns may be furnished to either spouse. Only one signature is required. Sign Form 4506-T exactly as your name appeared on the original return. If you changed your name, also sign your current name.

Corporations. Generally, Form 4506-T can be signed by: (1) an officer having legal authority to bind the corporation, (2) any person designated by the board of directors or other governing body, or (3) any officer or employee on written request by any principal officer and attested to by the secretary or other officer.

Partnerships. Generally, Form 4506-T can be signed by any person who was a member of the partnership during any part of the tax period requested on line 9.

All others. See Internal Revenue Code section 6103(e) if the taxpayer has died, is insolvent, is a dissolved corporation, or if a trustee, guardian, executor, receiver, or administrator is acting for the taxpayer.

Documentation. For entities other than individuals, you must attach the authorization document. For example, this could be the letter from the principal officer authorizing an employee of the corporation or the Letters Testamentary authorizing an individual to act for an estate.

Privacy Act and Paperwork Reduction Act Notice. We ask for the information on this form to establish your right to gain access to the requested tax information under the Internal Revenue Code. We need this information to properly identify the tax information and respond to your request. You are not required to request any transcript; if you do request a transcript, sections 6103 and 6109 and their regulations require you to provide this information, including your SSN or EIN. If you do not provide this information, we may not be able to process your request. Providing false or fraudulent information may subject you to penalties.

Routine uses of this information include giving it to the Department of Justice for civil and criminal litigation, and cities, states, and the District of Columbia for use in administering their tax laws. We may also disclose this information to other countries under a tax treaty, to federal and state agencies to enforce federal nontax criminal laws, or to federal law enforcement and intelligence agencies to combat terrorism.

You are not required to provide the information requested on a form that is subject to the Paperwork Reduction Act unless the form displays a valid OMB control number. Books or records relating to a form or its instructions must be retained as long as their contents may become material in the administration of any Internal Revenue law. Generally, tax returns and return information are confidential, as required by section 6103.

The time needed to complete and file Form 4506-T will vary depending on individual circumstances. The estimated average time is: **Learning about the law or the form,** 10 min.; **Preparing the form,** 12 min.; and **Copying, assembling, and sending the form to the IRS,** 20 min.

If you have comments concerning the accuracy of these time estimates or suggestions for making Form 4506-T simpler, we would be happy to hear from you. You can write to the Internal Revenue Service, Tax Products Coordinating Committee, SE:W:CAR:MP:T:T:SP, 1111 Constitution Ave. NW, IR-6526, Washington, DC 20224. Do not send the form to this address. Instead, see *Where to file* on this page.

EXHIBIT "B"

2632 COLLEGE PKWY • PO BOX 1706 • SCOTTSBLUFF NE 69363 1706
PHONE: 800.550.0508 • FAX: 303.728.3816

Making Home Affordable Program
Request for Modification and Affidavit
Addendum

Borrower Name(s): _____

Loan #: _____

Property Address: _____

Servicer: Aurora Loan Services LLC

If you have reported an amount in the 'Other' box on page 2 of the Request for Modification and Affidavit (RMA) under the Monthly Household Expenses/Debt column, please complete the table below to provide a breakdown of the expenses/debt provided in the 'Other' box. This itemization is necessary to ensure all appropriate expenses and debts are considered in our review of your HAMP Loan Modification request.

Itemization of 'other' Monthly Household Expenses/Debt	Monthly Amount
Food	$ 450.00
Utilities (electric, gas, telephone, cell phone, etc.)	$ 600.00
Transportation	$ See in P&L
Cable/internet	$ 100.00
Medical bills/Co-pay	$ 100.00
Insurance premiums (life, auto, etc.)	$ See in P&L
Any additional property maintenance costs	$ n/a
All non-HOA property dues or maintenance fees	$ n/a
Other: Misc Spending Money	$ 250.00
Other: Taxes	$ 1350.00
Other:	$
Total Other Expenses*	$ 2,750.00

* This total must match the amount in the 'Other' box on page 2 of the RMA under the Monthly Household Expenses/Debt column.

Signed:

_____   _____
Borrower   Date

_____   _____
Borrower   Date

_____   _____
Borrower   Date

_____   _____
Borrower   Date

⌂ Equal Housing Lender

INCOME/EXPENSES FOR HOUSEHOLD[1]

Number of People in Household:

Monthly Household Income		Monthly Household Expenses/Debt		Household Assets	
Monthly Gross Wages	$0.00	First Mortgage Payment	$ -	Checking Account (s)	$1,500.00
Overtime	$0.00	Second Mortgage Payment	$ n/a	Checking Account(s)	$
Child Support / Alimony / Separation[2]	$0.00	Insurance	$91.00	Savings/ Money Market	$0.00
Social Security/SSD	$1,177.	Property Taxes	$ -	CDs	$0.00
Other monthly income from pensions, annuities or retirement plans	$(spouse) 0.00	Credit Cards / Installment Loan(s) (total minimum payment per month)	$300.00	Stocks / Bonds	$0.00
Tips, commissions, bonus and self-employed income	$4,407.	Alimony, child support payments	$0.00	Other Cash on Hand	$250.00
Rents Received	$0.00	Net Rental Expenses	$0.00	Other Real Estate (estimated value)	$(500,000.)
Unemployment income	$0.00	HOA/Condo Fees/Property Maintenance	$0.00	Other ___	$0.00
Food Stamps/Welfare	$0.00	Car Payments	$See P&L	Other ___	$0.00
Other (investment income, royalties, interest, dividends etc.)	$0.00	Other See addendum sheet ___	$2,750.	Do not include the value of life insurance or retirement plans when calculating assets (401k, pension funds, annuities, IRAs, Keogh plans, etc.)	
Total (Gross Income)	$5,584.	Total Debt/Expenses	$3,141.	Total Assets	$498,250.

INCOME MUST BE DOCUMENTED

[1] Include combined income and expenses from the borrower and co-borrower (if any). If you include income and expenses from a household member who is not a borrower, please specify using the back of this form if necessary.

[2] You are not required to disclose Child Support, Alimony or Separation Maintenance income, unless you choose to have it considered by your servicer.

INFORMATION FOR GOVERNMENT MONITORING PURPOSES

The following information is requested by the federal government in order to monitor compliance with federal statutes that prohibit discrimination in housing. You are not required to furnish this information, but are encouraged to do so. The law provides that a lender or servicer may not discriminate either on the basis of this information, or on whether you choose to furnish it. If you furnish the information, please provide both ethnicity and race. For race, you may check more than one designation. If you do not furnish ethnicity, race, or sex, the lender or servicer is required to note the information on the basis of visual observation or surname if you have made this request for a loan modification in person. If you do not wish to furnish the information, please check the box below.

BORROWER	✓ I do not wish to furnish this information	CO-BORROWER	I do not wish to furnish this information
Ethnicity:	Hispanic or Latino / Not Hispanic or Latino	Ethnicity:	Hispanic or Latino / Not Hispanic or Latino
Race:	American Indian or Alaska Native / Asian / Black or African American / Native Hawaiian or Other Pacific Islander / White	Race:	American Indian or Alaska Native / Asian / Black or African American / Native Hawaiian or Other Pacific Islander / White
Sex:	Female / Male	Sex:	Female / Male

To be completed by Interviewer

Name/Address of Interviewer's Employer

This request was taken by:	Interviewer's Name (print or type) & ID Number
Face-to-face interview Mail	Interviewer's Signature Date
Telephone Internet	Interviewer's Phone Number (include area code)

EXHIBIT "C"

FINANCIAL HARDSHIP AFFIDAVIT

Borrower:
Account No.:
Address:

A. BACKGROUND

My former occupation was a real estate agent. With the advent of the real estate depression, I was no longer able to make a living. As a result, I became past due in my mortgage payments and received bad credit from all the unpaid bills and foreclosures.

My properties have either been foreclosed upon or are in the process of foreclosure. I can no longer count on any rental income because everything is in foreclosure. Also, I am not current on your mortgage but I want to come to an agreement with you on an affordable loan modification.

It is my sincere hope to save this home. I have had tremendous difficulty transitioning earning money in my career over the past two years. That's the reason that I have had difficulty paying the mortgage to you.

I am now working with a broker who has many contacts with bank foreclosure departments and I am getting to assist him to sell those homes. I expect a good increase in my income in the short term and the ability to pay an affordable mortgage on this house. I am now at the point of turning my finances around.

B. MY INCOME: My income is now sufficient to make timely monthly mortgage payments each month—if the scheduled payment were in line with my net income (what I can really afford to pay) and the present value of the home. My wife is 63 years of age and I am including her social security income of $1180. to help pay monthly expenses.

Since I am self-employed, you will see attached the "Year To Date Profit & Loss Statement" enclosed with this loan modification paperwork. You'll see that I am making better money now than I was six months ago.

C. YOUR LOAN: Your first trust deed is now approximately $475,000. The home directly next door with greater square footage is now on the market for a sales price of $250,000. and has not sold in over **6 months**.

Based upon present sales in the neighborhood, I would reasonably estimate that the home is now worth, **at the very maximum**, $225,000. on a "short sale" basis.

Auction value of the home would, as you know, be much less than $225,000., perhaps $150,000 or even less.

Also, I've been told that you can now rent a home like ours for no more than <u>$1500. a month</u> because of the depressed rental market in the neighborhood. I'm told that people just don't have the money now to pay high prices in the neighborhood for rent like they used to.

D. <u>MY REQUEST</u>: I respectfully request: (1) that you reduce my monthly payment, including taxes and insurance impounds, to no more than $1500. per month so that the home will be affordable to me and my family on a long term basis.

Thank You very much for your attention to this letter.

EXHIBIT "D"

To: Mortgage Company
From: _____
Date: _____

RE: Loan Number:
           Property Address:
           Financial Hardship Letter

Dear Sir/Madam:

I am writing this letter in the hopes of obtaining short-sale approval on the above-referenced mortgage loan held by --- Mortgage. I have found myself in a financial position that I had never anticipated and I am doing everything humanly possible to rectify the situation.

My monthly income has decreased due to ---

And my monthly expenses have increased due to ---

My household financial circumstances have changed due to --- (death in the family, serious or chronic illness, disability, divorce, incarceration, increased family responsibilities, etc...).

As is evident from the attached financial statement, I am unable to continue to make the monthly mortgage payments on the above-referenced real property. My cash reserves are nonexistent or insufficient to pay my mortgage and cover basic, daily living expenses, and my monthly debt payments are excessive and I am over-extended to my other creditors.

To compound my financial situation, my home will not sell in today's market for what I owe on the property and will sell for substantial less than what I even paid for it --- years ago. I have had my home listed for sale with a realtor for --- months. In that time we have had very little interest in the property and are grateful to have received any offer to purchase, albeit for less than what is owed.

I am requesting that you approve the short sale of my home as presented so that neither one of us continues to incur more indebtedness for this mortgage.

Very truly yours,

EXHIBIT "E"

FINANCIAL HARDSHIP AFFIDAVIT

Borrower:
Account No.:
Address:

A. BACKGROUND

I request a "deed in lieu of foreclosure" for the above referenced property. I have great financial hardship at this time. I am unable to pay the mortgage for this vacant home. I can deliver it to you quickly and in "broom swept" condition. There are no loans on the home other than your loan. It has already been on the market for sale through a local real estate broker for over 60 days and there have been *no offers* whatsoever.

My former occupation was a real estate agent. With the advent of the real estate depression, I was no longer able to make a living because I couldn't sell anything. As a result, I became past due in my mortgage payments and received bad credit from all the unpaid bills and foreclosures.

The properties that I previously owned have either been foreclosed upon or are in the process of foreclosure. I can no longer count on any rental income because everything is in foreclosure. In fact, you are seeking to foreclose on the home which is the subject of this request for a deed in lieu of.

Please review my credit report. When the 3 year lease to my automobile recently came due this Summer , my auto dealer would not give me a purchase loan to buy the car. In fact, I made numerous attempts to buy any car but no one would sell to me because of all my bad credit at this time. I must have filled out at least 5 loan applications to purchase a used car. I couldn't qualify even for a $5000. auto loan and that doesn't buy a lot of car!

As a result, I own no car of my own and am driving my wife's old 1997 Ford which has 135,000 miles, but drives dependably so I know I won't get stranded in the middle of nowhere. My wife is 65 years old and unemployed.

I have had tremendous difficulty transitioning into a new career over the past two years. At this point, I am now working as a part-time
employee to assist clients with their real estate closings. I attach a budget which shows what I am now earning. I don't have money to carry and pay for vacant houses any more.

The house which is the subject of your foreclosure suit is vacant and has been vacant for some time. There is no way that I can afford to pay $2400., the scheduled payment, or any payment at all under these circumstances. No one wants to rent the home because they know it is in foreclosure. Further, I wouldn't want to rent the home since you request that it be vacant in order to do a deed in lieu of foreclosure.

The highest rent I have ever received for this home is $1595. per month. I have to pay a local property manager 10% of the rents in order to manage the home so the real rent is closer to $1400. per month when its' occupied. So, under the most positive circumstances, there is a $1000. per month negative cash flow even when the property is rented.

I thank you very much for your attention to this letter.

www.ingramcontent.com/pod-product-compliance
Lightning Source LLC
Chambersburg PA
CBHW081226170526
45165CB00009B/2975